Spells
for
Teenage
Witches

Spells for Teenage Witches

Marina Baker

KYLE CATHIE LIMITED

To my mother, Margaret, the whitest brightest witch. Her kindness and spirit make the world a better place...

First published in Great Britain in 2000 by
Kyle Cathie Limited
122 Arlington Road
London NW1 7HP
general.enquiries@kyle-cathie.com
www.kylecathie.com

ISBN 1 85626 397 5

Reprinted 2000, 2001 (twice), 2002

Edited by Caroline Taggart
Designed by Mark Buckingham
Photography by Juliet Piddington
Styling by Wendy Deaner
Production by Lorraine Baird and Sha Huxtable

Marina Baker is hereby identified as the author of this work in accordance with Section 77 of the Copyright, Designs and Patents Act 1988.

A Cataloguing in Publication record for this title is available from the British Library.

Printed in Singapore by Tien-Wah Press

Contents

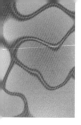

Introduction

Empower yourself through witchcraft. Seize responsibility. Act upon your desires to change your life and the world.

So long as your thoughts are pure and you mean no harm to others, the spells in this book can help you to do just that. Change the world. What this book cannot supply, however, is the most important ingredient of all: you.

You are the only one who can provide the imagination, strong will and belief to carry the spells off the page and into the cosmos where they may begin to work their magic.

How do magic spells work?

Magical power surrounds us. It may be found in everything from rocks and metal to wood, rainwater and a gentle breeze. Plus ourselves, of course.

We call this energy the fifth element, essence or, put most simply, Spirit. This Spirit is all powerful. It is the basis of life itself. It makes the planets spin, the tide come in, the sun rise and the seasons come round again. It also affects our moods and inter-actions – both with the world around us and between people.

If we can harness this power and channel it, we can use it to achieve great things. So how do we do this? To begin with we have to open our hearts and minds and acknowledge the Spirit.

We do this by focusing our attention on tangible objects known to contain the Spirit, such as candle flames, pebbles and flowers.

Other useful tools include coloured ribbons, crystals, rainwater and personal items such as hair or nail clippings. All pretty basic stuff, away from the context of witchcraft. But in the right setting – a spell – they act as a catalyst, allowing us to channel specific aspects of the Spirit.

This is achieved through help from God and Goddess. We are all familiar, I'm sure, with the concept of God. In witchcraft we have two Gods, one male, the other female. Hence God and Goddess. Which is how it should be. God and Goddess are not imbued with human qualities like the deities of Greek mythology, although we do sometimes call upon them, speak to them, as though they were almost human. This is more for our benefit, to help us express our needs.

The best way to envisage God and Goddess is as two unique energy sources. To aid visualisation we think of God as represented by the Sun and Goddess as symbolised by the moon. God and Goddess aren't actually the sun and the moon, of course. But the sun and moon are part of them. Understand this concept and you are well on your way to becoming a witch.

You also need to know about the four elements: fire, earth, water and air. Fire and earth are associated with the sun. Water and air are connected with the moon. Everything living depends on the elements. Without them, nothing could survive. In fact, the world would not exist, since the elements make up the very fabric of our entire existence. The elements are the world.

Meditate a moment on the significance of the four elements – how they work together, their potential use to us – and you

begin to understand their importance. And why, therefore, witches hold them in such high esteem.

Witches realise that objects such as candles, stones, flowers and rain not only represent the elements, they are of the elements. And each element contains the Spirit which is part of the whole Spirit. Thus when casting a spell, assuming it is cast well – which requires thought, respect and a cast-iron belief in our abilities – witches have the entire energy of the universe at their disposal. And nothing on earth comes more powerful than that.

Uphold the Witch's law we must,
In purest love and earnest trust.
Please think before a spell's begun:
"If I harm no one, then no harm is done.
For what I do comes back to me,
Multiplied by the power of three."
If followed with your mind and heart,
We'll merry meet and merry part.
If followed with your mind and heart
We'll merry meet anon.

Casting a Circle

Casting a circle before a spell is an important ritual. This mental and physical preparation helps you to be focused and will have a positive effect on your magic.

To this end, before casting, make sure you are unlikely to be disturbed and if necessary give the room a quick tidy, to minimise chaotic influences.

Next lay out the tools and ingredients needed on the altar. This should lie from east to west, allowing you to face north. Directions may be determined with a compass.

Hold your wand out from your body, pointing northwards. Visualise a white light emanating from your wand and walk slowly in a clockwise direction.

As you walk say:

"This circle is a positive field, a protective shield."

Walk the circle a second time, saying:

"This circle keeps me safe within, no harm can enter in."

Walk the circle a third time, saying:

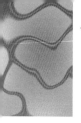

"This circle will enhance my spell ensuring that I cast it well."

Facing north, trace a pentacle (see page 12) in the air with your wand. Do the same to the east, south and west.

To open a circle at the end of a spell, point your wand northwards and walk the circle in an anti-clockwise direction, saying:

"I do not break this circle but the circle is undone.
The spell that I have cast it has begun.
Mindful of the witch's rede
Now the magic has been freed
I will harm none.
Yet if harm's done
It shall return by the power of three."

Note that witches working in the southern hemisphere prefer to cast their circle in an anti-clockwise direction and open it clockwise.

Commonly asked questions

This section should answer any questions you may have arising out of the spells in this book – and a few others besides.

What should I wear?

Casting a spell is a special occasion, so why not dress up? You should keep an outfit specifically for wearing when working your magic. It doesn't have to be bought especially or expensive. It should be clean, not something you have been wearing all day, and loose fitting – comfortable, in other words.Don't go for something long and flowing with big sleeves, since these can get in the way, and when working with candles could present a hazard. For the same reason, if you have long hair, tie it back.

Where do I get hold of things like crystals, shells, ribbons, etc?

Most of the ingredients used in these spells may be found. Candles, ribbons essential oils and burners can be purchased from good department stores. Crystals are often sold in specialist shops – either geological or pagan.

Where do I find a wand?

You will find the right wand for you when you go looking for it. Hazel is the best, although oak, rowan and apple may also be used. So it is helpful if you look beneath these trees. A twig might have fallen naturally from the tree or be hanging off, waiting for you to come along. If you don't know your hazel from your apple, get your hands on a book that can help you to decipher the various species.

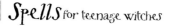

What is a pentacle?

It is a five-pointed star representing the four elements and the Spirit. It should lie in the centre of your altar for all spells unless otherwise stated. Pentacles can be bought, but they can just as easily be made.

Take a pair of compasses and draw a circle. Keeping the compasses open at the same distance (i.e. that of the radius of the circle), place the point of the compasses on the perimeter and make a mark to create a cross on the edge of the circle. Put the compasses point in the middle of the cross and make another mark. Continue to do this all the way around the circle.

You will now have five crosses. With a ruler, draw a line to link up every other cross. When completed you will have a pentacle.

For spell use, you can make a pentacle out of stiff card or, if you have access to the right equipment, from clay or wood.

What do I need for an altar?

A small table or chest is suitable. This should be covered with a white cloth kept specifically for this purpose.

Don't witches need bonfires? We only have a communal garden where I live. What should I do?

None of the spells in this book involves lighting fires. They are unnecessary. Candles will provide all the power of the fire element needed for your magic.

How do I melt wax?

Stand a pudding bowl in a saucepan containing 5cm/2in of water. Put the candle or candles in the bowl, which should be reserved for this purpose thereafter. Place over a medium heat and the wax will melt.

Melted wax is hot. Do not put your fingers in it, and be very careful when carrying the bowl, since you don't want to spill the contents. Depending on room temperature plus the size and quality of the candles, the wax may be moulded when it has stood for about 20 minutes to half an hour. Stir with your wand occasionally during this time. When you come to mould it, test it tentatively to ensure there are no hidden pockets of hot wax that could burn you.

It goes without saying that melting wax is an activity that should be avoided when there are young children around. Accidents can happen and an unfortunate youngster could be scarred for life. Remember once again, if you harm no one no harm is done.

How do I burn sage?

If picked fresh, dry the sage out for at least a day. Use a taper to light it, then blow gently to extinguish the flame. It should then smoke for a few minutes and go out of its own accord.

If it continues to burn for longer than is required by your spell, set it down in a heat-proof dish such as a clay bowl.

These instructions also apply when using a bunch of sage bound with cotton thread. Take seven sprigs and tie at the bottom end. Wrap the thread around them towards the end of the leaves, then back again and tie.

As with candles, do not leave burning sage unattended.

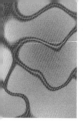

How do I get hold of hair or nail clippings from somebody else?

You will have to use your initiative on this one. Once you have got hold of it, place it in a small pill-box, so that you don't muddle it up with other specimens.

What if I don't have candles or threads in the right colours?

Go and find them. Colour is important. Did you know that the colours we can see with the naked eye – those of the rainbow – form only a small part of the entire colour spectrum? The reason we can see rainbow colours is that our eyes have the ability to read the frequencies. It's a bit like an AM radio. Any number of radio shows may be broadcast in the vicinity, but an AM radio can only pick up AM frequencies.

The "colour" frequencies that we can't see include X-rays – beyond the violet end of the spectrum – and microwaves at the other end. Radio waves occur further along the red end.

Make an effort to find the right ingredients. You might not fully understand the principles of colour use in spells, but you'd better believe that the Spirit does.

Here is a simplified table of the significance of colour as used in this book:

red	health, strength, protection, vitality, creativity
pink	love, romance, honour, morality, friendship, compassion
orange	energy, assertiveness, endurance, encouragement, adaptability, stimulation, fire, to seal a spell
yellow	intellect, confidence, communication, eloquence, movement, happiness, success, self-esteem, attraction
blue	protection
green	prosperity, finance, luck
light blue	healing, peace, patience, friendship, understanding, protection of home, water, air
purple	healing severe disease, spirituality, meditation, inner power, tension, ambition
brown	animals, comfort, security, home, uncertainty, earth
indigo	deep relaxation, restful sleep, charity
silver	intuition, dreams
dark blue	impulsiveness, depression, changeability
dark purple	negativity, change, release, renewal, chaos, confusion, protection

Do I need to join a coven to become a witch?

No. It is only since the middle of the last century that witches have opted to work in groups, called covens. But it has always been, and most definitely still is, perfectly acceptable to work alone. If you have contact with other young witches via the Internet, you can work simultaneously to lend a spell your combined strength.

If you know of other aspiring young witches in your area, there is no reason why you can't pool resources occasionally without forming a formal coven. The witches sabbats provide a perfect opportunity for you to get together – you will find more about them on pages 86-94. After a rite, you can let your hair down and party. There is a spell in this book to ensure that such a gathering is successful (see page 60).

When a *spell* requires me to bury or hide something, when do I open the circle?

Open it before you move from the spot where the spell was cast. The burial or hiding is actually an affirmation, for your benefit as much as for the elements and the God and Goddess.

Good witch practice

1 Wish no harm on others. Be aware that harm may be caused unintentionally. Observe this number one rule, and the rest should fall into place.

2 Keep matches, oils, candles, etc in a safe place where small hands can't get hold of them. Out of sight is not enough. They should be stored out of reach.

3 Candles should be placed well away from curtains, plants, papers or anything else which might catch light. Never ever leave candles burning unattended.

4 When out collecting material for your spells, take a friend or responsible adult with you. Make sure your parents or carer know where you are and at what time you expect to be home. If you change your plans, call and tell them.

5 Never embark on a spell that requires bathing if you are particularly frazzled and exhausted. Falling asleep in water is highly dangerous.

6 If a particular plant grows in abundance it is probably okay to pick a few flowers for a spell. But some species of wild flowers are protected and should be left alone. If at all possible, take plants from sustainable sources, such as your own garden or houseplant collection.

7 Essential oils should never be applied directly to the skin unless diluted in the correct proportion with a base oil. Oils should never be ingested. Ensure the water used is warm and do not allow the dish to burn dry. Always use a tea light candle in a metal case with a burner.

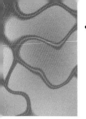

first spell: find the Spirit

A self-initiation. Accomplish this task and you may begin to call yourself a witch. For once you have found and acknowledged the Spirit, you have the power to cast a spell.

Don't worry if you find this spell difficult. Visualisation takes practice. It could take weeks to really feel you have transported yourself and opened up your senses to the elements. But it is well worth the perseverance.

an oil burner • 3 drops of lavender oil

Sit cross-legged, hands resting on knees, palms facing upward. Close your eyes.

Breathe in deeply through your nose, then out through your mouth. Do this until you relax and clear your mind of thoughts.

Now imagine yourself alone somewhere beautiful. A mountain. A beach. Woodland. Transport yourself there in your mind.

Ask yourself, what is the weather like? Warm sunshine? A strong breeze? Is it raining? How does this feel on my skin? What can I smell? Salt air? Flowers? Soil? What can I hear? Bird song? Waves? The rustle of trees?

Contemplate the nature of the elements and how fire, earth, water and air all play their part in this environment.

In your own time, return to the oil burner. Consider how each element is represented and how they work together.

Keep breathing in through your nose and out through your mouth. When you truly understand, you may lift your arms, palms facing upwards, and say:

"I acknowledge the presence of the Spirit. I am its servant and its keeper. I may use its power to do my will, so long as none is harmed and it be the Spirit's will."

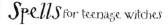

Lucky charm

a small stone with a hole in it • green ribbon

Thread the ribbon through the stone and tie three knots to secure it. Then chant:

"Imbue this stone with luck for me, multiplied by the power of three. God and Goddess hear my plea. If it be your will, then let it be."

Wear the stone around your neck.

Good fortune accumulator

a crystal • an egg cup • a small bowl • a larger bowl • a jug of rainwater

Place the crystal in the egg cup, then put the egg cup inside the small bowl and the small bowl inside the larger bowl.

Pour water over the crystal until it just overflows from the egg cup, saying:

"The divine powers of the God and Goddess protect me.
May their kind benevolence seek help from the Spirit in the elements."

Pour more water on to the crystal until the water overflows into the larger bowl, saying:

"Harness their potency, God and Goddess,
send joy and good fortune to bless me."

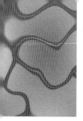

Mega success spell

1 green leaf . **1 yellow flower** . **1 blue flower** . **a handful of earth** . **a bowl** . **an orange envelope**

Hold up the green leaf with your right hand, saying:

"This green leaf brings me luck."

Still holding the leaf, pick up the yellow flower in the same hand, saying:

"This yellow flower bestows success."

Pick up the blue flower in the same hand (holding on to the others), saying:

"This is for the Spirit by whom this spell is blessed."

Place them in the bowl and scoop up the earth, saying:

"I sprinkle with our mother's earth,
a reminder that I still
must work extremely hard
if I'm to have my will."

Look at the bowl and repeat this rhyme twice more. As you do, imagine yourself engaged in the activities necessary to achieve your goal (such as studying or practising).

Place the flowers and soil in an orange envelope, seal it and store it somewhere safe. Whenever you feel the need for a top-up, hold the envelope between the palms of your hand and repeat the evocation three times.

The great savings spell

You believe you would be happier if you were richer and yearn for a spell to prove it. But money spells must never be taken lightly. Think carefully about where a fortune might come from. Suppose it appeared in the form of an inheritance on the death of someone special?

Like all the best spells, here's one for financial gain that involves some discipline and application on your part.

3 gold coins (they don't have to be real gold) . a green envelope . some gold thread . rainwater

Place the coins in the envelope and seal it.

Wrap the gold thread around the envelope, saying:

"This thread will bind both coins and mind.
This thread will bind both coins and mind.
Save I will and spend I might,
but saving is both true and right."

Bury the coins and sprinkle with rainwater. When you feel a spending urge coming on, return to the spot and sprinkle with rainwater, while chanting:

"The thread it bound both coins and mind.
The thread it bound both coins and mind.
Save I will and spend I might,
but saving is both true and right."

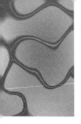

Anti-hex

If you appear to be overrun with bad luck or you don't seem to be getting on with people, maybe it is because someone is wishing you ill.

If this cannot be resolved through friendship, or you don't know who is responsible for your troubles, try this spell.

a small apple twig • a hair from your head

Wrap the hair around the twig, saying:

"Whoever it is that vexes me,
could vex themselves by the power of three.
As I wish them no harm, I'll bind their power
to the safety of a neutral tree."

Place the twig and hair in the branches of a nearby tree.

Spell in a bottle

Send good fortune out into the world. It might make some lucky person's day. You will also benefit, since all the magic you send out returns to you multiplied by the power of three.

a sturdy clear glass bottle • a cork • yellow paper • light blue and green ink • lavender oil • purple ribbon

This spell is best performed around the time of a full moon, on a trip to the coast. Using the blue ink, draw Celtic spirals in each corner of the paper. In the centre of the page draw an Egyptian ankh cross (see illustration opposite). Around it in a circle, using the green ink, write:

"Finding this charm brings you great fortune. To release the magic, hold your hands up to the sea, saying: 'Thank you, Spirit, for blessing me.'"

Sprinkle three drops of lavender oil on to the paper, roll it up tightly and secure with the purple ribbon.

Slide it into the bottle and seal with the cork, saying:

"Mother Goddess, watch over this charm.
Urge the elements to ease its passage towards the one who will look and find.
And let this person greet the message with open mind so they might benefit from your blessing."

Throw into the sea as the tide is going out.

Good mood in the morning

An essential spell for all you grumps out there who haven't a pleasant thought or word to share with others before lunchtime.

jasmine oil* . **a silk handkerchief**

Pour five drops of jasmine oil on to a burner. Stand up straight, feet slightly apart. Stretch up to the ceiling and bend over to touch your toes. Do this seven times. Jog furiously on the spot, counting to 14. Touch your toes another seven times. Jog on the spot counting to 21.

Pour three drops of oil on to the handkerchief and carry it with you all day. Now eat some breakfast and cheer up.

* Jasmine oil is very expensive. It costs five times as much as many oils for half the amount. But in this instance it may be a worthwhile investment for both you and your family. Buy the real thing. Often jasmine is diluted to bring the price down. Such oils might create a nice scent, but they are not as effective at altering one's mood.

Revision spell

3 drops of geranium oil for girls or bergamot oil for boys
• oil burner • a crystal

Sprinkle the oil on to the burner.

Sit cross-legged on the floor, a crystal in front of you, with your hands resting on your knees, palms up.

Take a deep breath in through your nose for seven counts. Breathe out through your mouth for seven counts. Do this seven times.

Imagine golden rain falling down on you, washing away your tiredness and stress. When you are ready, say:

"My mind is empty. My soul is free from the stress and worry that make me weary. God and Goddess, now hear my plea: give me the strength, vigour and courage to study. I will learn. I will remember. My knowledge will grow. If it be your will it will be so."

Say this 3 times.

Repeat the breathing.

You are now ready to work.

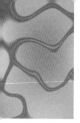

Study buddy talisman

So long as you don't distract each other, a study buddy makes revision and homework easier. When you make a commitment to sit down with your books, you are more likely to do so. Plus, you can help one another with testing and explanations. Trying to disentangle another's confusion often sorts it out in your own mind. And once you understand something, you are far less likely to forget it.

2 good-quality yellow candles – 1 for each of you
- **light blue, pink and purple ribbons plaited to form a cord**
- **objects you have collected on a walk with your friend**

When studying together burn half a yellow candle. The next time you meet up, burn half of the other candle

When you can afford the time, skip a study session and go for a walk instead. If you live in a town, find a park. If you are fortunate enough to live near a beach, woodland or the foothills of a mountain, go there. You can still test one another as you walk.

Look around for interesting objects, such as leaves, feathers, flowers, small shells or pieces of bark. You will know what you're looking for when you find it.

Back home, melt both halves of the candles according to the instructions on page 13.

Cast your circle and work within it. When the wax is cool enough to handle, divide it in half and form two balls. Mould each one to form a heart. Then decorate with the bits and pieces from your walk.

Before the wax hardens too much, pierce each heart and thread the cords through, saying:

"I invite the Spirit to come to us, to bless us with the presence of God and Goddess. At work and at rest may they lend us strength to complete the tasks that are set for us."

Open the circle, and wait until the wax is totally hard before attempting to hang up the hearts – one in each of your homes.

Even when you have to study alone, you will be reminded of each other's endeavours and feel spurred on to do better.

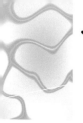

Invisi-spell

Unprepared for a lesson? Dreading being called upon to speak in class? Chant the following while staring directly at the teacher:

"God and Goddess hear my need
and understand why I must plead
for magic shafts of astral light
to hide me from this teacher's sight.
I haven't done the work, you see,
so please don't let them pick on me.
Guide them to a mind so bright
they'll surely find the answers right."

Handwriting spell

This spell dates back to the second century AD. More recently the word abracadabra has been hijacked by conjurers who say it with gusto while pulling rabbits out of top hats.

Forget that. Traditionally the word is believed to hold great healing and changing properties. Because it is so powerful, it is helpful to anyone whose handwriting resembles the work of a maniac spider let loose with a bottle of ink.

white paper • indigo ink • white ribbon • sticky tape

Using the paper and ink, copy out the following by hand (do not type it):

$$
\begin{array}{c}
A\,B\,R\,A\,C\,A\,D\,A\,B\,R\,A \\
A\,B\,R\,A\,C\,A\,D\,A\,B\,R \\
A\,B\,R\,A\,C\,A\,D\,A\,B \\
A\,B\,R\,A\,C\,A\,D\,A \\
A\,B\,R\,A\,C\,A\,D \\
A\,B\,R\,A\,C\,A \\
A\,B\,R\,A\,C \\
A\,B\,R\,A \\
A\,B\,R \\
A\,B \\
A
\end{array}
$$

Fold the paper in four, roll it around the ribbon and secure with sticky tape.

Tie the ribbon around your neck and wear it as a talisman for nine days. Then, rising early, go to a river or stream. Slide out the ribbon and without opening the paper toss it over your shoulder into the water.

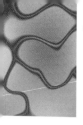
Rainy spell

Originally an Indian charm for bringing on the rainy season, this updated version is useful for avoiding outdoor sports, or for getting a lift to school. But mindful of the witches' law, please consider the damage or disappointment a downpour or lightning might cause to others.

a blue candle (birthday-cake variety) • a bowl of rainwater • dark blue paper

Place the candle in the cauldron, ensuring you don't get the wick wet. Tear up the paper and float the pieces on the water. Light the candle while chanting the following:

"Nimbostratus, cumulonimbus
bring me the jewel of rain
nimbostratus, cumulonimbus
only for a day
nimbostratus, cumulonimbus
bring me the jewel of rain
nimbostratus, cumulonimbus
then please roll away."

Chant until the water snuffs the candle out.

Sunny Spell

Most cultures have magical rites to control the weather. This one is based on an Inuit practice, where the wind is called to the fire. Once the air is contained within the two elements, of earth (candle) and fire (flame), it is extinguished with the fourth – water. This balance ensures minimal disruption to other areas. But there will be some. For if you get your dry day (don't expect to create a heat wave) it will probably rain somewhere else instead.

Taba is an Inuit expression meaning "It is enough."

rainwater . a lighted white candle in a jar

After casting your circle, lift your arms skywards, saying:

"Taba taba taba wind. Taba taba taba. Leave the storm you brew. Come warm yourself by the fire."

Lower your hands slowly until they point to the candle.

"Come in to the fire. Come in."

When you feel that the wind has answered your call, throw water over the candle, saying:

"I mean no harm to anyone and call upon the Spirit to ensure no harm is done. To the four elements I give thanks. Let me now welcome the unhindered presence of the sun."

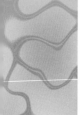
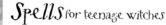

Bully freeze

dark purple paper • **white chalk** • **light blue ribbon** • **access to a freezer**

Using the chalk, write the bully's name on the paper, then draw a vertical line down through the name.

Roll up the paper to form a scroll and tie with the ribbon.

Open the freezer and deposit the scroll, saying:

"Freeze (name of person), freeze.
This bullying must cease.
You will not bother me
and you must now go in peace."

Close the freezer and visualise the bully losing interest and all fear draining from you.

Sunrise Spell

To be performed first thing – as the sun rises – on a big day. You might have an important test, an audition or an interview. Perhaps you are moving home or changing schools. This spell ensures that you are able to make the most of new and important situations.

As the sun rises, go outside and face eastwards. Standing on one leg and using your arms to balance you (hold them out in an upward-pointing V-shape), lift the other leg in front of you. Sweep it around to the side and then the back. Repeat standing on the other leg.

Do this seven times before holding one leg up and balancing as motionlessly as you can. Should you begin to wobble, pull in your tummy and imagine a thread leading from the top of your head up into the sky, holding you up, like a marionette.

When you feel your fingers tingling – and they will – say:

"I am at one with the all-powerful essence.
I thank you, God and Goddess, for the gift of your presence.
I welcome the Spirit into me, lending wisdom and energy.
With your help I can achieve to the best of my ability."

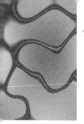

full moon spell

If you were able to fly around in space, you could view a full moon every day. The moon herself never changes. Her waxing and waning is an illusion created by her changing position in relation to the earth and the sun..

So why should a full moon be any more important than a crescent moon? Well, in one sense it isn't. The moon is the moon is the moon. Yet a full moon provides light. In the days before electricity and street lighting, a full moon was an important source of illumination. You could harvest and hunt by it, so man and woman's survival depended on it.

But the practical benefits of a full moon in no way detract from the importance of planetary positions. The gravitational pull of the moon is highly influential, affecting everything: the weather, the sea, plants and us – our bodies are, after all, made up of 90 per cent water. Many farmers understand that planting crops around a full moon can help seedlings grow.

This same power can be utilised to strengthen our magic. The following spell can help you tune in and harness this energy. But all the spells in this book may be enhanced when cast around a full moon.

a crystal • **a pentacle** • **a wand** • **dark purple candles in jars**

Outside at night, place your pentacle on the ground with the lighted candles on either side. Hold the crystal in your left hand and the wand in your right. Hold both arms up to the moon, saying:

"Glorious Goddess, I bathe in your beauty, energy and light. I acknowledge the magic of this night, the ecstatic spirit of your might. While I may never fully understand the mysteries of your powers, Great Mother, grant me permission to share in your gift. Empower me to help others."

The moon is always beautiful. Spare a moment every evening to find her in the sky and marvel.

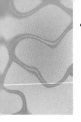

Birthday spell

1 tree

Stand under the tree, staring up at the branches, admiring its shape, colours and texture. Give the tree a big hug, saying:

"We're another year older, you and me.
I am human. You are a tree.
But the Spirit joins us so hear my plea:
may each new ring bring wisdom to me."

Sleepy Spell

Cast this spell just before bedtime. It will help you to put your worries and troubles to one side in order to obtain a good night's sleep. You will awake refreshed and more able to take on the world. Dried hops may be bought at specialist herb shops, health food shops or anywhere that supplies home-brewing kits.

muslin cloth . indigo ribbon . a few drops of lavender oil . an oil burner . a cup of dried rose petals . a cup of dried hops . a cup of dried mint leaves . a cup of dried rosemary

Light the oil burner and sprinkle on the lavender oil. Place the dried herbs in the muslin and wrap them up like a parcel. Secure with the ribbon, saying:

"Goddess of the night skies, I call upon your powers to make a garland of the stars and set it gently down to rest upon my shoulders. Let serenity soothe my eyes and clear my mind. May a deep sleep rise and pass the time till morning lights the skies, when I might wake refreshed and by your spirit blessed."

Place the parcel under your pillow when you go to sleep.

Anti-cramp Spell

I suffered from terrible night cramps during my teens. This cure was suggested by a close relative. Because it is a traditional "folk" remedy, you need not cast a circle for this one.

a cork from a wine bottle • pale blue thread • red thread

Tie the threads around the cork and place under your pillow.

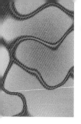

Once~a~month 1

Period pain – or cramps or dysmenorrhoea – can be so disruptive. Low back ache, abdominal pain, nausea and possibly faintness make it difficult to get on with life.

If you suffer in extreme, tell your doctor about it, in case there is an underlying medical condition that needs attention. But in most cases, period pain is simply the result of being a young woman – nothing we can do about that, sorry! But anxiety and stress certainly exacerbate the problem. This we can do something about.

There is no need to cast a circle for this folk spell. But you may like to light a coloured candle of your choice, place it on the corner of the bath and gaze into the flame to aid relaxation.

3 drops rosemary oil • 2 drops peppermint oil

After running a warm bath – don't make it too hot or you might begin feeling dizzy and flushed – drop the oil on to the water and stir with your hand. Keep the bathroom door closed to keep the fragrance in the room.

Lie in the bath breathing in through your mouth and out through your nose. As you breathe in, imagine the air going to your tummy and lower back. As you breathe out, feel the pain leaving your body through your mouth.

When you have had a good soak and are beginning to feel more "human", pull the plug out first, then get up slowly. You don't want to faint, especially into a full bath.

If you are suffering from faintness and nausea, use a hot-water bottle and heat the oil on a burner instead.

Once-a-month 2

5¹/₂ teaspoons hazelnut oil • 10 drops rosemary oil • 10 drops peppermint oil • 10 drops sage oil

Rub this massage oil around your hips, lower back and abdomen for 1 minute. Do this every day for 5 days, from when your period begins.

It is particularly helpful after taking a warm bath (see Once-a-month 1, opposite).

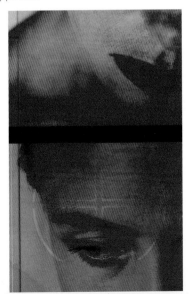

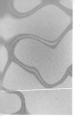

Vice Spell

No matter how hard you wave your hazel wand, this spell, like all the others, will not work unless you truly desire a positive outcome and believe it is possible. Not easy, no, when we're talking about a vice, such as nail-biting, squeezing spots, smoking or watching too much television. You know you shouldn't, yet you continue to do it all the same. But when you feel a moment of great mental fortitude coming upon you, cast this spell and give up your bad habit. For good.

1 jar with a lid • the thing you want to give up or a token of it • a sprig of dried sage • dark purple ribbon • a dark purple candle

Light the tip of the sage with the flame from the candle (read the instructions on page 13 first).

Walk around within your circle in a clockwise direction so that you become surrounded by a plume of sage smoke.

Place the token on the inside of the jar lid. Hold the jar upside down over the sage. When the jar fills with smoke, pop the lid on. Bind the jar closed with ribbon saying:

"God and Goddess, bless my presence of mind.
Give me the courage to recognise that I chose to end this vice.
Should I be tempted to yearn, then more sage I will burn."

If temptation raises its head, repeat the spell using a new jar. Should you soon find yourself with three bound jars, bury them in the garden and try the Changing Spell (see page 61) before returning to this one at the next full moon. Now you have embarked on this course of action, you must keep trying to stop.

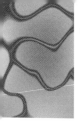

Tidiness spell

Can you hardly get in to your bedroom for the mess? Do you have trouble jamming your school locker shut before half the contents spill back out on to the floor? Oh dear. You sound just like the old me.

Tidiness is a wonderful thing. An uncluttered environment aids concentration, relaxation and a good night's sleep. It also makes finding things much easier.

When you resolve to change your ways, don't attempt the whole clean-up operation in one go. Start with your storage areas, such as drawers, shelves and the wardrobe Empty these out one at a time and make three piles: one of things you want to keep, one of objects you're not sure about and a third for the stuff you must throw or give away. Sort through the second heap again, putting everything in either the first or third pile.

Everything you are keeping should be put away again. You may now start on the floor and, if you're feeling brave enough, all that junk under the bed. You may even feel inspired to do the same thing with your school locker.

In the meantime, try this spell. I'm afraid you will have to clear a good-sized portion of the floor first.

a packet of sea salt • a handful of lavender flowers • a large bunch of sage, bound together with blue thread (see instructions for burning sage on page 13)

After casting your circle, waft the sage in a spiral motion, saying:

"Chaos be gone from here. Pandemonium's rule now ends. Let the elements weave their energies through this room to clear and cleanse."

Open the circle and sprinkle salt and lavender on the floor. Go to each corner of the room and clap your hands loudly, while calling out dynamically:

"Go! Go! Go!"

The following day, clear up the salt and lavender and get sorting!

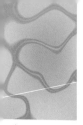

Shiny Shiny

Witches use herbalism as well as magic to have their will. Try my mother's old recipe to give tired hair a new lease of life.

half a bottle of your favourite shampoo • a large bunch of rosemary • a large bunch of nettles (use gloves when handling) • a large bunch of mint • 150ml/¹/₃ pint boiling water • muslin cloth

Place the cloth over the bottom of the bowl with the edges lapping over the sides.

Place the herbs on the muslin and pour the water over them.

Leave to steep for 30 minutes.

Pick up the corners of the muslin and squeeze out the water.

Using a funnel, pour the liquid into your shampoo and shake to mix. Wash your hair with it in the normal way

Irresista-spell

Best performed on a full moon at midnight.

1 small seashell • pink cloth • a hair from your head • orange ribbon

Place the shell and the hair in the cloth.

Close your eyes and imagine yourself surrounded by golden light.

Tie up the cloth with the ribbon. Keep the pouch on you at all times and you will charm everyone you meet.

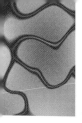

The butterfly spell

Are you constantly late for everything? Do you never seem to have the right things with you? This organisation spell is for you.

2 rose petals • relaxing instrumental music (Tibetan is very good) • 2 orange candles impregnated with lavender oil (dip the wicks in the oil and wipe some over the candles)

Play your music, at a low unobtrusive volume.

Having cast your circle, lie down on the floor between the two candles – each 30cm/1 foot away from your head – and place the petals over your eyes.

Breathe in deeply through your nose and out through your mouth seven times.

Visualise an orange golden light rising from your toes, up your body to your head. Imagine you are a cocooned caterpillar. Gradually feel your arms developing into beautiful large butterfly wings.

As they grow, the cocoon splits open and you emerge into bright sunlight.

Take to the air, looking down on a flower-filled enchanted garden.

Come to land on a red rose. As you sit there, warming your wings, count backwards slowly from 21, continuing to breathe as instructed.

Say gently to yourself:

"I am changed because I wish to be.
The only person barring me from change was me.
I lacked consistency.
But now I am free to be
the being I want to be.
I am a new me."

Keep lying down and breathing for as long as you wish. Get up very slowly and open your circle. With your brand new frame of mind make an orderly list of things to do tomorrow. Include one treat for yourself and one good deed for another.

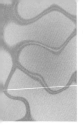

Notice me spell

Think long and hard before embarking on this course of action. Question your motives. Why do you desire this person so badly? Why do you suppose they have not fallen for you of their own accord? Are they involved with someone else? Are you both entirely unsuited? And remember that using magic on others may not have the effect you desire. They are, after all, their own person. Be careful what you wish for and be prepared to deal with the consequences, should your spell be successful.

a nail clipping or hair from the person you admire • a red wax candle • black thread • a nail • white cloth

Melt candle wax as instructed on page 13. When it begins to solidify, mould into a ball before casting a circle. Press the nail clipping or hair into the wax, then shape it into the person's form. Tie one end of the thread round the effigy's waist and the other round the nail. Twist the nail in a clockwise direction so that the thread winds around it, saying:

"Come (person's name), come to me.
You don't know why but can't deny
your need to come to me.
My thoughts are pure and free from sin
but with this thread I draw you in.
Feel the pull of destiny.
Come (person's name), come now to me."

Wrap the nail and wax model in white cloth and store them somewhere safe, so that there is no chance of anybody tampering with this powerful spell.

Obsession mandala

The Tibetans, one of the most spiritual of cultures, understand that nothing lasts forever. They create intricate sand mandalas to bring about change, then pour them away into a river. If you are besotted by someone to the point of distraction, or are trying to get over an ended relationship, make your own mandala.

a round tray • dry sand • dough made from flour, tea and butter, kneaded and formed into 4 little cakes, all bearing your own and the other person's initials • a handful of grain, such as wheat or barley • a drum

Pour sand on to the tray. Use your finger to write the name of the person you need to cast out from your mind. Decorate around it with swirls and flourishes. Different coloured sands may be used – be as elaborate as your resources allow.

Place the cakes around the edge to form the corners of a square within the circle. Sprinkle the grain over the mandala. Bang the drum. Feel guided by the Spirit as you vary the rhythm, tone and volume. Over this shout or chant:

"Change brings change and change brings change.
Nothing lasts, nothing is forever."

When you feel sufficiently confident that you can take this idea on board, proceed outside and scatter the mandala.

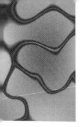

Love nurture

1 carefully weeded small plot of earth about 40cm/15in square somewhere hidden but not too dark • 1 packet grass seeds • 1 forget-me-not plant • stones and shells

Use your wand to trace a heart shape 35cm/13in across. Place stones around the edge.

Trace the initials of your loved one in the centre of the heart and fill in with shells.

Sprinkle the grass seeds within the stone boundary and water them. Plant the forget-me-not within the heart.

Tend every day, weeding and watering as necessary.

As the grass grows, it may be trimmed to keep it even.

Should you wish to call it a day on the relationship, pull out the forget-me-not and cut the grass back hard.

Three days later remove the shells and stones and scatter them somewhere they will do no harm.

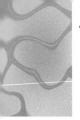

Hands off

If you are subjected to unwanted physical attention, you are totally within your rights to tell the person concerned where to go. If you don't feel able to do this, talk to someone else about it instead. Tell a responsible adult what is happening. Don't think you have to protect anybody by keeping quiet. They have betrayed your trust by their actions. Put an end to the situation now. Speak out.

If it is more a matter of someone having a simple crush on you, ease them down gently with this spell.

a lock of hair from their head • a small piece of red paper • black ink • a nail • a hammer

After casting the circle, write the person's name on the paper using black ink. Wrap the person's hair in the paper. Place the paper on the ground, somewhere secret. Bang the nail through the paper into the ground, saying:

"I mean you no harm.
But I bind you still to leave me alone.
It is my will."

Please don't shout

Do your parents seem unable to sit down and discuss their differences like grown-ups? It might be tempting to get involved, shout as loudly as they do, take sides. But let's not. Instead, wait until the kitchen is clear, melt your wax, then take yourself off to your bedroom and cast this spell.

2 small pieces light blue card • purple ink • 1 good-quality white wax candle • 50cm/20in light blue thread • a hair from each of your parents' heads (check out their hair-brushes and combs if you don't want to ask them directly)

Heat the wax according to the instructions on page 13. When it has cooled, divide it in half and mould two figurines, one obviously male and the other female. Wrap the hair around each head, ensuring you get the right hair for the right figure.

Take the light blue thread and tie one end round each model's waist. Lay the thread out straight on the floor. Then gently begin rolling the figures towards each other – until they are close together and facing one other – saying:

"Please don't shout, Father and Mother. Please don't shout. Talk to each other."

Store the figures in a box where they won't be disturbed.

On each of the cards write: "Please don't shout. I love you." Then sign your name. Hide one in the pocket of a coat belonging to each parent. They will find them soon enough.

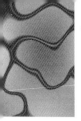

family home charms

Families come in all shapes and sizes. In a dream world every child lives with both parents as one happy family. But life for many of us is not like that. If you have lived as one family group, separation or divorce can be particularly hard because you know what you are now missing. And whichever parent you stay with, it just doesn't feel like home any more.

Make these charms and hang one in each of your parents' dwellings. They will remind you that you now have two family homes. You are welcome, loved and protected in both. The magic should rub off on your parents, too, ensuring they can at least be civil to one another in your presence.

This spell is also useful if your parents have been apart for years, or always. And if there are step- or half-brothers and sisters involved, this will help you all to feel part of the same family.

6 small seashells for each family member, including siblings, step- and half-siblings • 2 larger seashells for each person • 2 tiny bells for each person • 2 smallish pieces of driftwood (about 21cm/9in long, or a bit more if you have a large family) • light blue thread

Find shells that already have holes in them. Do not attempt to pierce them yourself.

After casting your circle, begin threading the shells, leaving a 4cm/1½in gap between each. Two shells should be followed by the bell, followed by the next small shell, then the large shell, which will hang at the bottom of the thread.

Leave enough thread at the top, say 21cm/9in, to attach each strand to the driftwood about 5cm/2in apart. When you have finished you will have two almost identical charms, both with the same number of strands. Step- and half-siblings should be included on both charms, even if they spend time in just one home.

Use more thread to create a loop to hang them up in a window at each home.

As you work, meditate on your parents' relationship and ways you can help your family to get along together more positively.

When you hang the charms say:

"I call upon the elements to banish insecurity, quell discord and adversity.
Allow the Spirit to connect us as a family wherever we may be.
Help me to understand I am not alone.
I am home. I am loved. I am home."

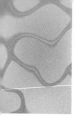

fantastic party spell

friends • food • beverages • a selection of flowers from
your garden (if you don't have a garden ask friends to bring
flowers with them) • yellow candles • lavender oil

Invite your friends around for a party. Call it a celebration of
friendship. You might hold it on your birthday or on a full moon,
or some other important day such as one of the witches' sabbats
(see pages 86–94).

Display the flowers in vases around your home. Place candles in
secure holders. Ever mindful of safety, ensure that the candles
aren't placed anywhere that presents a fire hazard (see Good
Witch Practice, page 17). Pour a few drops of lavender oil on to
a lighted burner.

Just before you expect the first guests to arrive, step outside the
front of your house. Hold your hands up to your home, saying:

*"Spirits bless this party. May everyone who comes discover new
friendships and rekindle old ones. May all these kindred souls
find joy in my home. And when the feast is done and it's time to
part, may they carry the party away in their hearts."*

Changing spell

a piece of pliable willow • a small bell • yellow, brown and white thread plaited to form a cord • a sprig of dried sage

Attach the bell to the cord and use to bind the willow to form a closed circle, like a bracelet. Wear it on your right wrist. Light the sage (read the instructions on page 13 first). Once it is burning, blow out the flame and hold the sprig in your right hand. Swirl it in an anti-clockwise direction before holding it still and asking yourself the following three questions:

"What do I want to change?"
"Why do I want to change this?"
"What is the best solution to bring about change?"

Take time in between each question to allow the answers to form in your mind.

After opening your circle, display the bracelet where you can see it, to remind you to act upon the decisions you have come to.

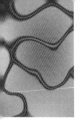

forgiveness from the skies

Your mind continues to return to an old argument. The actions of another made you so angry. But isn't it time to move on? Friendship is invaluable. Bearing grudges wastes energy. Shed the burden of troubled thoughts with this spell.

a mirror • pink flowers • rainwater • a blue sky

Lay the mirror flat on the ground so that it reflects the sky. Lay the flowers on the mirror and sit cross-legged beside it.

Hold your palms out towards the flowers and channel all your negative energies towards them.

Sprinkle water on to the flowers, saying:

"Time moves in circles.
We move on the wheel.
Anger be gone.
The rift must heal."

Hold your hands, palms up towards the sky, saying:

"Now my heart is open to positive energies.
Our bond is restored, our friendship revitalised."

Before opening your circle, make a pact with yourself to do something special for this friend. And don't be surprised if your change of heart requires some getting used to on their part.

When your friendship is back on an even keel, if you think it is appropriate, do the spell together.

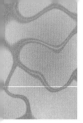

Whiter than white spell

If you have developed a reputation that you feel is unfounded, or that no longer suits you, casting this spell will improve your public image.

3 small white pebbles • 3 white flowers • white ribbon • 3 white candles • a hair from your head • a jar of runny honey with a third removed

Set the candles out on your altar to form a triangle pointing northwards. Place the jar of honey in the middle. Touch the pebbles with your wand, saying:

"Three pebbles pure and white,
lend me purity to set my image right."

Pick up the flowers, saying:

"Three flowers pure and white,
bestow your innocence,
lend me your light."

Put the flowers and pebbles into the honey with your hair. Wrap the jar in the white ribbon, saying:

"I have regrets, I have done wrong.
But now I sing a different song.
I cause no trouble, I am no rebel.
This ribbon binds, my whiteness trebles."

Store the jar out of harm's way. If life gets tricky, undo the ribbon and retie, chanting the spell again.

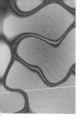

Green fingers spell

Do you garden? A good witch should. A simple window box or a few houseplants provide a good way of getting started, instilling confidence before you move on to a flowerbed or vegetable patch.

Find a simple textbook that explains the basics. Really, it doesn't have to be complicated. Plants need water, sunlight, the right-sized pot and nourishment. Precise requirements vary with each species. Through careful observation, you will soon recognise when a plant needs more water, less sunshine, etc.

Tend your plants well and you will be working in harmony with the Spirit. As the seasons pass, you will be able to study the rhythm of life at close quarters.

Such an experience can only fill you with wonder at the workings of nature. Grow herbs and you can provide some of the ingredients for your spells.

a rosemary plant • a lavender plant • a sage plant
• 3 seashells • 3 pebbles

In a window box or a round tub: layer crocks (broken bits of flower pot) on the bottom to aid drainage and plant the herbs in a good potting compost.

Secure well on a window ledge or in a sunny spot outside – partial shade is acceptable, but it should receive full sunlight for a period each day. Hold up the shells and pebbles, saying:

"From the sky above and the earth below,
I call upon the Elements,
to help these plants to grow.
Spirit, breathe magical life into all I sow."

Place the shells and pebbles on the soil, saying:

"God and Goddess, bless this effort with success."

Each time you tend your plants, chant: *"Blessed with success"* three times.

If you have to go away, make sure your plants' needs are still catered for. And sing them a song before you leave. Plants love being sung to.

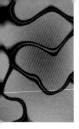

Squabbling siblings peace spell

a magnet for each sibling, including yourself • a hair from each of your heads • a small light blue candle in a jar

Place the magnets together, trapping your hairs between them. As you do this, say:

"We're bound together by the hair.
No more cries of 'That's unfair.'
No more squabbles, no more fights,
we'll live in peace with love and light."

Bury the magnets in the ground and place the lighted candle in its jar above it. Repeat the chant and meditate on your siblings' good points and ways you can help them to love you.

Ill feelings dispelling spell

dark purple thread • white candle

Tie a separate knot in the thread for every embarrassing or annoying incident you wish to put behind you. If it is something that you regret, say: *"I forgive me"* as you make a knot. If it is the action of another, say: *"I forgive you"* as you meditate on what has upset you.

Wrap the thread tightly around the white candle, 2.5cm/1in from the top.

Light the candle.

When the wick has burned down through the thread, these troubles are behind you.

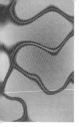

Rainbow peace spell

This spell may be done alone, but you may also invite close friends to join you. Your collective powers, even if others are not practising witches, will give the spell added momentum. And let's face it. Peace has yet to be given a chance. Humanity needs all the help it can get.

1 flower in each of these colours: red, orange, yellow, green, blue and violet • 1 white ribbon to bind the flowers in a posy • a candle in each of the rainbow colours to match the flowers

Sit in a circle, facing inwards and holding hands, within the circle you have cast. Whoever organised the spell acts as the high priest or priestess. Light the candles, saying: *"Each candle I light, I light for peace."*

All say: *"Bring peace. Bring peace. Bring peace."*

You say: *"Red, to comfort those who suffer in grief."*
All say: *"Bring peace. Bring peace. Bring peace."*

You say: *"Orange for the war weary."*
All say: *"Bring peace. Bring peace. Bring peace."*

You say: *"Yellow for those with injuries."*
All say: *"Bring peace. Bring peace. Bring peace."*

You say: *"Green for those who negotiate."*
All say: *"Bring peace. Bring peace. Bring peace."*

You say: *"Blue to quell the anger of those who violate."*
All say: *"Bring peace. Bring peace. Bring peace."*

You say: *"Violet for all who wish an end to hostilities."*
All say: *"Bring peace. Bring peace. Bring peace."*

You say: *"These flowers are a gift from the Spirit in all things. May the Spirit in return send the world a blessing. An end to war. An end to suffering. A future of hope, love, peace and happiness blessed by God and Goddess."*
All say: *"Bring peace. Bring peace. Bring peace."*

Leave the candles to burn down. After opening your circle the flowers may be laid under a tree that is special to you. Whenever you see a rainbow, say: *"Bring peace. Bring peace. Bring peace."* Close your eyes for a moment and will it to happen.

If everyone did this spell, there would be no one left to fight. If you have contact with other witches, via the Internet or by phone, tell them when you intend to cast this spell and suggest they work at the same time.

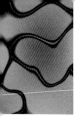

Psychic development

Psychic ability means more than being able to see into the future or know what someone is thinking. Really, it is about you being in touch with the Spirit. This is a most important aspect of witchcraft. It is what powers the spells.

This is why many spells require a degree of contemplation not unlike the exercise below, the accepted basic meditation for improving psychic awareness.

Psychic proficiency will also be improved by the following measures: exercise frequently, eat a healthy, balanced diet, keep houseplants or take up gardening and get out into the countryside as often as you can.

From time to time you can test your aptitude. Gradually you should see a marked improvement on your score. To send a message telepathically is as much of a skill as receiving one. So don't forget to take it in turns.

25 postcard-sized white cards • a black marker pen • a friend

At sunset – outside if weather permits and you are likely to be undisturbed – sit comfortably, with your back straight and your hands resting, palms up, on your knees.

Breathe in through your nose and out through your mouth until you are relaxed and focused. Imagine a golden light emanating from your solar plexus as you breathe in. Feel that this light is full of love.

On your in breaths, say to yourself: "Spirit."

On your out breaths, say: "Energy."

This should take about 15-20 minutes.

Then, to test psychic capabilities, choose five symbols, such as two wavy parallel lines, a triangle, a square, a star and a cross. Draw each image five times so that you have one image on each of your 25 cards.

Shuffle them up and get a friend to study one symbol at a time. As they do this, draw whichever image comes into your mind.

Repeat with the whole deck.

By the law of averages you should get five right. Any more correct answers may be attributed to a psychic connection.

Alternative peace spell

an act of kindness • an orange candle

After lighting the candle, sit cross-legged on the floor, breathing in through your nose and out through your mouth.

As you stare into the flame, make a pact with yourself to initiate an act of kindness today. Help someone less fortunate than yourself. Smile at somebody, say thank you. Open a door and allow a person to pass in front of you.

As His Holiness the Dalai Lama of Tibet once said: "The key point is kindness. With kindness one will have inner peace. Through inner peace, world peace can one day be a reality."

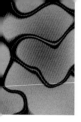

Cold spell

We all catch colds from time to time. And they can make you feel wretched. The best way to ensure your body can cope is to eat a healthy, balanced diet, including lots of fresh fruit and vegetables. You should also exercise regularly, as this strengthens the immune system.

But if you are feeling under the weather, the following spell should help. The healing powers of tea tree and eucalyptus have been known to the Aboriginal tribes of Australia for thousands of years.

3 drops of tea tree oil • 2 drops of eucalyptus • red cord

Heat the oil on a burner. Tie seven knots into the cord. With each knot say:

"God and Goddess, have pity and heal me."

Tie the cord around your wrist.

The following day, heat more oil and undo one knot, saying:

"God and Goddess, through your power I am healed."

Repeat until the knots and the cold have gone.

Occasionally a cold can lead to complications. Contact a doctor immediately if your cold is accompanied by two or more of the following symptoms: high temperature, chest pains, a stiff neck, headache or a rash resembling bruising that doesn't fade when pressed.

Seashell Spell

For a friend or relative with a serious illness.

20-30 seashells • 5 purple flowers • access to a safe sandy beach as low tide is turning to come in (by safe I mean one where you won't be cut off by the incoming tide)

Face the sea and draw a pentacle in the sand with your wand.

Press a purple flower into each point of the pentacle.

Using the seashells, write the initials of the person who is ill in the middle of the pentacle.

Chant three times:

"I call on the Spirit, the fifth essence, to bless you with a presence.
Air bring strength, fire bring rest, earth lessen pain and water cleanse.
When comes the sea, by the Spirit let it be
that you are healed by the power of three."

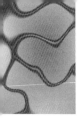

fellow traveller spiral spell

Very occasionally you meet someone special. They're just so easy to get along with. You share a sense of humour. Your interests are similar. You speak the same language.

Such a moment is rare. For you have met a fellow traveller in this world. This spell celebrates your friendship, and ensures you gain wisdom from the knowledge of one another.

a pentacle • pink paper with your names on it, decorated with a Celtic spiral • a spiral seashell • a small pebble • a feather • a small candle • a homemade white cloth bag

After casting the circle, light the candle.

Touch the pentacle with your wand and say:

"I call on the Spirit in all things to bless my friend. Goddess of the moon, care for them. God of the sun, protect them."

Hold the pebble at a safe distance above the candle. Move it in a clockwise spiral three times, saying:

"May they find comfort in the earth."

Take up the shell and repeat the spiral motion, saying:

"May the sea give them courage and serenity."

Do the same with the feather, saying:

"May the wind lend them strength and cleanse their heart."

Do the same with the paper, saying:

"May the fire warm their hearth and light their path."

Place the objects in the bag, saying:

"In all these things may they feel the Spirit. And as these gifts are blessed by God and Goddess, so too is our friendship. Fluid as the water, bright as the flame, light as the air, deep as the earth."

Whenever you want to send warm vibes to your friend, sit cross-legged on the floor and lay the objects out in front of you. Circle your hand in a spiral motion above them, saying:

"I send you love from the beginning to the end.
As our paths have crossed so our souls must blend.
I send you love and blessings, friend."

Then imagine a great energy emanating from your being and spiralling around your friend.

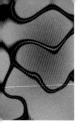

Bereavement spell

Only when you can accept that a loved one has gone from our world can your heart begin to heal. You may be thinking: "If only there was a spell that could bring them back." Yet imagine if there was such magic. The world would be overrun with all manner of pain and suffering.

Some people find it helpful to discuss their feelings. Others prefer not to because the very person they would talk to is also distressed by the death and they don't wish to upset them further.

At such times you might try a spell for sleeping, or one for family unity to encourage support.

The following, however, is a spell that allows us to acknowledge a death, to let go of the person and find strength to continue with our own lives. You can do this spell days, weeks, months, even years after a bereavement. Only you will know when the time is right, to set their spirit free to soar.

an oil burner • a few drops of lavender oil • 1 purple candle • light blue paper bearing the person's name and three reasons why you miss them, written in indigo-coloured ink • a fireproof bowl • a sprig of rosemary

Light the oil burner and sprinkle oil on to the water before casting your circle. Light the candles, saying:

"From the north, the east, the south and west, come water, fire, earth and air. "

Place the paper in the bowl and use a candle to set it alight, saying:

"I release the spirit of (person's name) to your eternal care."

Imagine the person smiling, bathed in golden and mauve light.

Place the rosemary in the bowl saying:

"With this gift of herb their memory is sealed,
in the knowledge they are free and I will be healed."

Scatter the ashes and rosemary somewhere special within 24 hours. As you do, repeat the charm.

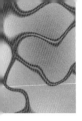

The blessing of the unicorn

Perform this spell on the night of a full moon.

7 oak leaves • a bath • a white robe • 2 drops of frankincense oil • 3 drops of lavender oil • 3 white candles (placed at the 3 corners of a triangle, pointing northwards) • a pentacle (placed within a triangle) • 3 oak twigs bound with white ribbon• a crystal

Before casting your circle, drop the oak leaves into a warm bath and soak yourself. As you lie there, close your eyes and imagine a white light above your head. Feel the warmth of the glow gently sliding down over your face and head, your neck, shoulders, arms, chest, hands, fingers, waist, hips, groin, thighs, knees, calves, ankles, feet, toes, chest.

As the light reaches each part of your body, feel all tension melting away. Then ease the light into your mind, emptying your head of all thought. DO NOT FALL ASLEEP.

Leave the bath, dry off and put on the white robe.

Heat a few drops of frankincense and lavender oil on a burner.

Cast your circle. Light a candle and, raising the crystal in your left hand, touch the pentacle with your wand, saying:

"Goddess of the moon, I call on you.
God of the sun, I call on you.
Let the dark shine light, let the light shine dark.
Fire from wood and wood from fire
wind arouse and waves subdue.
God and Goddess, I call on you."

Place the crystal and wand on either side of the pentacle, take the twigs in both hands, kneel and say:

"By this gift from the God and Goddess I summon the Unicorn.
If it be their will you will come to me in radiant purity."

Place the twigs in your lap, open your palms upwards and with your eyes closed await the blessing of the Unicorn.

When you go to sleep, place the twigs beneath your bed for the sweetest dreams.

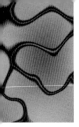

Quell the fire

an amethyst crystal • a hazel wand • a lake • a hazel wood • 2 apples, one with a moon symbol carved into it, the other with a sun symbol

"I went out to the hazel wood, because a fire was in my head," wrote the Irish poet W B Yeats, who was well aware of the magical potential of hazel. These beautiful trees act as natural conductors for negative energy, the kind that fills your head with dark thoughts, anger, unhappiness, confusion.

The hazel wood Yeats had in mind is on the outskirts of Sligo town in the west of Ireland. You would be fortunate to have a similar wood near you. If it happens to nestle on the shores of a shimmering lake, you would be blessed indeed. Aided by the water, a great cleanser, the amethyst attracting positive energies and the wand to harness the power of the woodland, anything is possible. The fire will subside.

If no hazel wood and lake are available, meditate on the potential of this spell and wait. I went out to Yeats' hazel wood, years after I first heard about it. That day it poured down with rain, which amplified the forces at work. It changed my life and was well worth waiting for.

Stand on the lake shore, amethyst in your left hand, wand in your right. Breathe in through your nose and out through your mouth. As you breathe in, feel nature's Spirit entering. As you breathe out, feel a greater power leaving, taking the fire with it. You should feel a tingle as the energies build up and up until it seems that your breathing controls the wind, the ripples on the lake, the movement of the trees.

Do this until you feel totally at one with your surroundings, connected to the Spirit in all things. Continue for as long as you desire. How you respond further to this amazing experience is a very personal thing. You will know what to say and do when the time comes.

Before leaving, place the apples in a tree as a gift.

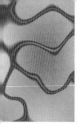

The witches' sabbats

Sabbats are celebrations, rites, festivals, that mark the changing seasons. The four greater sabbats are Imbolg, Beltane, Lughnasa and Yule.

Some witches have very complicated ceremonies that they perform on these days. In the formal setting of an adult coven, it is their prerogative to celebrate as they see fit. But so long as you give some thought, during the day, to the importance of the date, it is enough just to celebrate the occasion with a themed gathering of friends.

The one exception is Imbolg, a quiet private time, and one of great importance in the witches' calendar because of its associations with death and rebirth.

Also included here are ideas for Midsummer and Samhain (what now tends to be called Halloween). These are known as the lesser sabbats, along with the Spring and Autumnal equinoxes on 21 March and 21 September respectively. There are no traditional rites for these last two. They simply mark the quarter-years between the Summer Solstice (Midsummer) and Winter Solstice, or Yule.

You may acknowledge the equinoxes, if you wish, by renewing your last New Year's resolution. The Great Savings Spell (page 24) or Vice Spell (page 44) may be of use to you here.

Imbolg – 2 february

A celebration of light and the coming of spring, Imbolg marks the end of winter, a time when life begins to stir in the previously barren earth.

3 black candles • a crown of silver stars (made from silver foil and attached to white ribbon) • black and white ribbons twined around your wand • some early spring flowers and greenery – snowdrops, crocus, catkins, leaves, etc • a shawl • a handful of porridge oats • a broom

Light the candles, then sprinkle the oats on the floor. Take up your wand, saying: *"From darkness comes light. From night comes day. From winter and death come spring and life."*

Set the wand down, put on the crown and the shawl, then take up the flowers, saying: *"Girl in the moon, see off the darkness and let the light in."*

Touch the crown, saying: *"Mother in the moon, disperse death and raise life."*

Touch the shawl, saying: *"Wise grandmother in the moon, end the winter and begin the spring."*

Sweep up the oats, saying:

"Although you be three, you also are one.
As I begin to sweep the room, so have your powers begun
to banish the winter gloom,
welcome spring's flourish and nature's bloom."

Put the oats outside, as a gift to the birds.

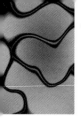

Beltane - 30 April

A celebration of summer's beginning. This ritual should take place outside – preferably on a hill – before sunset.

a group of friends • a piece of flapjack for each friend, carried in a single cloth bag • flowers for your hair • 13 tea-light candles in jars • a taper • 1 free-range organic egg

Flapjack is easily made. This recipe makes about 30 portions. Melt 375g/12oz butter. Stir in 450g/1lb rolled oats and 375g/12oz soft brown sugar. Press into a greased and lined tin, then bake at 180°C/350°C for 20-25 minutes. Cut into squares while hot and allow to cool in the tin before turning out on to a wire tray.

At this point place one piece back in the oven and cook until it blackens around the edges. When it has cooled, put it in the bag with the other flapjacks.

The Beltane ritual can now commence.

Set the candles in their jars in a circle and light them using a taper – the best way to ensure you don't burn your fingers.

Holding hands, dance or skip around a circle. Then take it in turns to enter the circle and jump over the candles. The higher you leap, the more success you will have in the following year.

When you have all had a go, sit down and pass round the bag, each of you taking a piece of flapjack. Whoever gets the burned piece has to jump three times over the candles while the person who made the flapjack throws the egg at them. If the cook gets the burned piece, the person on their left gets to throw the egg.

If the egg misses, the person jumping will experience great fortune in the coming year. If it hits home, each person must give them a small gift, to lend them the luck they appear to be lacking.

Please note, use cold water to wash egg out of your hair. Otherwise you will be picking bits of scrambled egg off your head for days after.

Midsummer – 21 June

The Sun God is at his zenith. The longest day and shortest night. Another perfect excuse for a party. If weather, circumstances and grown-ups permit, hold it outdoors.

Place an outdoor candle on either side of your front door so that guests must walk between them as they enter. If you live in an apartment opening on to a corridor, use tea-light candles in jars.

Near the door, have a bowl ready containing water and floating rose petals. Dip a sprig of heather into the water and, as you greet your friends, use it to sprinkle them.

At nightfall, bite into an apple while looking into a mirror. It is said that the man or woman you will one day marry will appear to you. I doubt you will actually see their face, but open your mind and you might well experience something of their personality.

If you can, stay up all night and greet the waning year with the Sunrise Spell (see page 37). At dawn you might also bathe your face in the morning dew. This is purported to be good for improving the complexion.

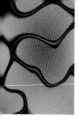

Lughnasa – 31 July

The end of summer, the beginning of autumn. We honour the harvest with a picnic and a good stiff walk up a mountain. Or a big hill with a good view of the surrounding area.

Organise yourself properly with suitable walking shoes and waterproof clothing. Get friends and family involved for a fabulous day out in the countryside. Do not go alone. Use public footpaths and don't stray from them. Tell a responsible adult what time you expect to return home. And stick to your word. Close gates after you and take all rubbish home.

You will need some good music for dancing and a lightweight portable CD or tape player, but please think of others, who may have climbed the mountain in search of silent solitude. You will also need a pot for collecting blackberries or bilberries. Don't pick either unless you are entirely sure you have the right fruit.

Eat them with cream and sugar when you get to the highest point. Then dance off the calories. Your picnic should also include apples and soft white rolls.

Leave plenty of time to get off the hillside before nightfall.

Samhain – 31 October

What a coincidence. This ancient rite falls on the same night as Halloween, the most Pagan, along with Christmas, of all the traditional Christian holidays. It is also the nearest thing we have to a national witch day.

Okay, so images of hags on broomsticks and bubbling cauldrons are not what we understand witches to be. But don't knock it. Samhain provides another perfect party theme. Carve stars, moons and spirals on a hollowed-out pumpkin. And please don't throw the flesh away. It makes wonderful pie and soup. Recipes are not difficult to track down at this time of year.

Have bowls of nuts and fruits available for your friends and for anyone who comes trick or treating.

This is also the night we remember the dead. Light a candle for someone no longer with us. Sit quietly for a moment recalling your fondest memories of them and tell them that you still love them and miss them very much.

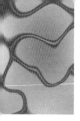

Spells for teenage witches

Yule – 21 December

The shortest day and the longest night. The wheel has turned, the days begin to lengthen.

This is the time when the Sun King is reborn, protected by the Mother Goddess. Decorate a tree in their honour.

Don't opt for shop-bought seasonal baubles. Create your own. Red ribbons may be tied in bows. You can make stars, spirals and moons out of shortcrust pastry: bake them and paint them gold and silver. Shells and bells may be strung together and strewn across the branches. You don't need to cut a tree down for this. You could deck out a handsome specimen in your garden.

Place a single candle in your window. Deck your room with holly. And yes, put a big star on top of your tree. A star, is after all, a sun. Just not the nearest one to our planet.

Throw a party and invite your guests to come dressed as suns and moons.

Last word

You cast a spell
And all being well
Your magic is a great success.
So offer praise where praise is due –
Say to yourself: "Well done you."
Yet never forget that you were helped
By the Spirit, God and Goddess.
Spare a moment to express your gratitude.
Call on them and say: "Thank you."

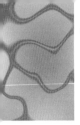
Acknowledgements

The author would like to thank the following fellow travellers for their help in writing this book: Pepper, Charlie and Bo, Rosie, Jo, Emma and Stevie Boy, Justine, Mike and Sarah H, Vicky B and Alice, Sarah D, Zaz, Wendy, Ruth, Abby, Yael and Matt, all the Saltdean mothers, Justin and Sharon, Martin and Beck, Rhianwen, Catherine and Seb, Ed, Caroline, Janet, Eileen and Steve O'Mara, Kate West and Brendan Dowling.

The quotation from W B Yeats' "Song of the Wandering Aengus" from **The Wind Among the Reeds** (1899), which appears on page 84, is reproduced by permission of A P Watt Ltd, on behalf of Michael B Yeats.